MACHINES CLOSE-UP

MILITARY FIGHTING MACHINES

Daniel Gilpin and Alex Pang

WAYLAND

This edition published in 2009 by Wayland

Wayland
Hachette Children's Books
338 Euston Road
London NW1 3BH

Wayland Australia
Level 17/207 Kent Street
Sydney, NSW 2000

Produced by

David West Children's Books
7 Princeton Court
55 Felsham Road
London SW15 1AZ

Designer: Gary Jeffrey
Illustrator: Alex Pang
Editor: Katharine Pethick
Consultant: Steve Parker

A CIP catalogue record for this book is available from the British Library.

ISBN: 9780750260749

Printed in China

Wayland is a division of
Hachette Children's Books,
an Hachette UK company.
www.hachette.co.uk

PHOTO CREDITS :
Abbreviations: t-top, m-middle, b-bottom, r-right, l-left, c-centre.
4-5, 30b, US Army photo; 7ml, Bundesarchiv; 30t, Danie van der Merwe; 30l, C. Todd Lopez US Army

CONTENTS

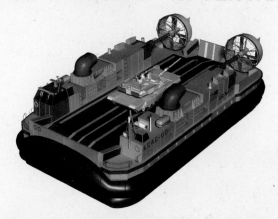

INTRODUCTION

The core of any armed force is its soldiers, but in the modern battlefield they are supported by a variety of military machines. These range from troop transporters to mobile heavy artillery. Most of these vehicles incorporate the latest in weapons and armour technology.

ADVANCING ARMOUR
Tanks have become an integral part of most nations' land forces, combining speed and manoeuvrability with awesome firepower.

HOW THIS BOOK WORKS

MAIN TEXT
Explains the history of the vehicle and outlines its primary role. Other information, such as which forces use it, is also covered here.

SPECS
This panel gives information about the vehicle's speed, dimensions, and operational range.

INTERESTING FEATURES
This box contains a detailed illustration of the engine or another design feature that makes the vehicle unique. Informative text explains the feature's function.

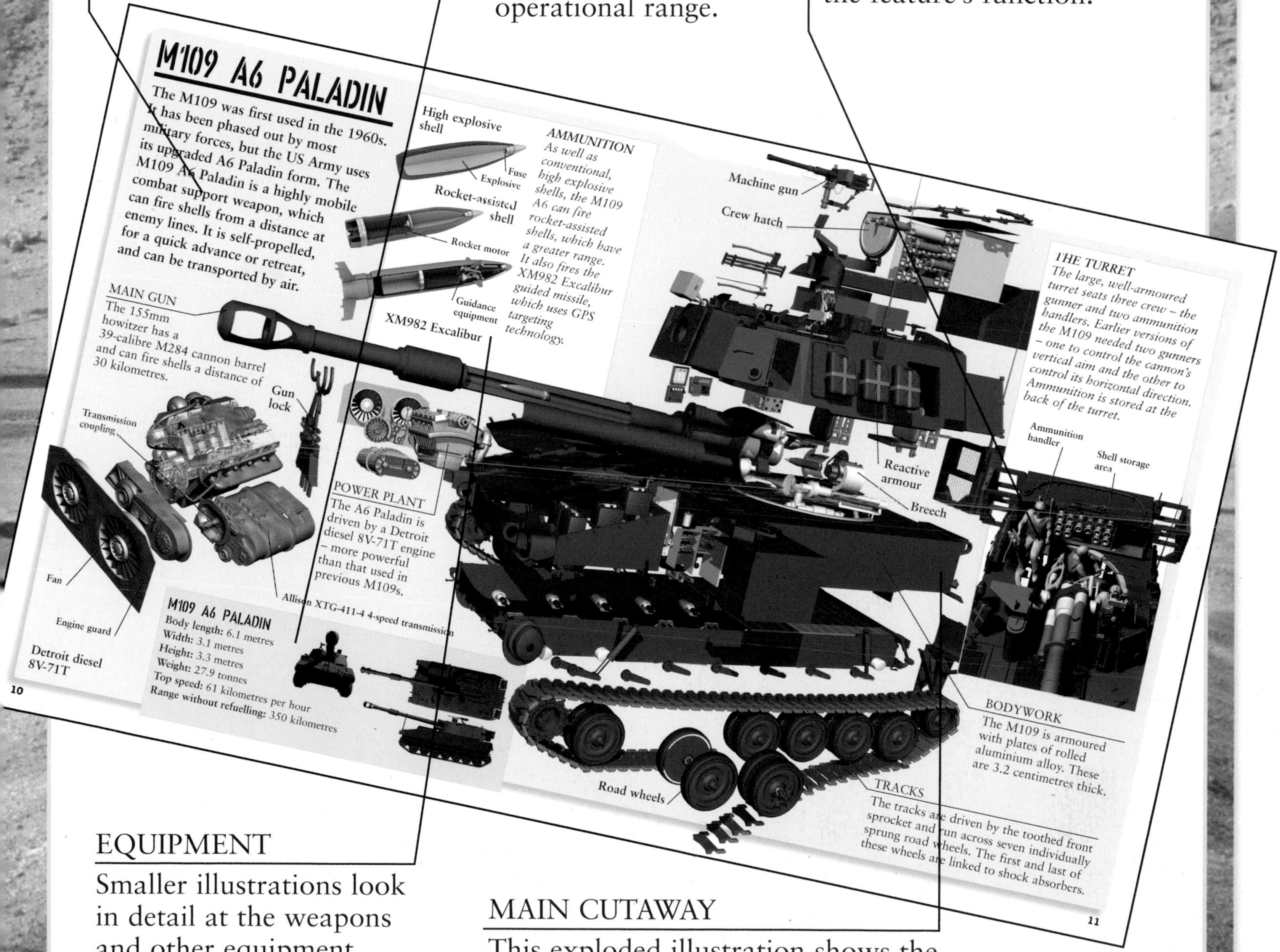

M109 A6 PALADIN
The M109 was first used in the 1960s. It has been phased out by most military forces, but the US Army uses its upgraded A6 Paladin form. The M109 A6 Paladin is a highly mobile combat support weapon, which can fire shells from a distance at enemy lines. It is self-propelled, for a quick advance or retreat, and can be transported by air.

MAIN GUN
The 155mm howitzer has a 39-calibre M284 cannon barrel and can fire shells a distance of 30 kilometres.

Gun lock

Transmission coupling

Fan

Engine guard

Detroit diesel 8V-71T

POWER PLANT
The A6 Paladin is driven by a Detroit diesel 8V-71T engine – more powerful than that used in previous M109s.

Allison XTG-411-4 4-speed transmission

M109 A6 PALADIN
Body length: 6.1 metres
Width: 3.1 metres
Height: 3.3 metres
Weight: 27.9 tonnes
Top speed: 61 kilometres per hour
Range without refuelling: 350 kilometres

High explosive shell

Fuse

Explosive

Rocket-assisted shell

Rocket motor

Guidance equipment

XM982 Excalibur

AMMUNITION
As well as conventional, high explosive shells, the M109 A6 can fire rocket-assisted shells, which have a greater range. It also fires the XM982 Excalibur guided missile, which uses GPS targeting technology.

Machine gun

Crew hatch

THE TURRET
The large, well-armoured turret seats three crew – the gunner and two ammunition handlers. Earlier versions of the M109 needed two gunners – one to control the cannon's vertical aim and the other to control its horizontal direction. Ammunition is stored at the back of the turret.

Ammunition handler

Shell storage area

Reactive armour

Breech

BODYWORK
The M109 is armoured with plates of rolled aluminium alloy. These are 3.2 centimetres thick.

Road wheels

TRACKS
The tracks are driven by the toothed front sprocket and run across seven individually sprung road wheels. The first and last of these wheels are linked to shock absorbers.

10

11

EQUIPMENT
Smaller illustrations look in detail at the weapons and other equipment carried by the vehicle to fulfill its different roles.

MAIN CUTAWAY
This exploded illustration shows the internal structure of the vehicle and gives information on the positions of its various working parts.

MOBILE ARMOUR

The history of armoured motorised vehicles dates back to World War I. That conflict witnessed the introduction of the tank – a vehicle that changed the way wars were fought forever.

BRITISH MARK VI TANK
British forces were the first to use tanks. Developed, surprisingly, by the Royal Navy, they were initially known as 'landships'.

GERMAN A7V TANK

DEVIL'S CHARIOTS

Tanks quickly earned a fearsome reputation. Although slow and cumbersome they were virtually impossible to destroy. Caterpillar tracks enabled them to span trenches and smash through barbed wire, while offering infantrymen a moving shield from enemy fire. By the end of the war more than 6,000 tanks had been built.

ARMOURED CAR
Vehicles like this were used early in World War I, before warfare from fixed trench lines took over.

RENAULT FT-17
Introduced in 1917, this was the first with a fully rotating turret.

LIGHT TANKS

Smaller and faster than the first tanks, these were pioneered mainly by the French, who made more tanks than anyone else in World War I.

LIGHTNING WAR

Having proved their usefulness in World War I, tanks were a feature of World War II from its beginning. It was Germany that took the lead in their design and development.

GERMAN SD KFZ 250 APC

PANZER IV
This was the only German tank to be produced all through World War II.

SHERMAN TANK
From 1942, this was the main tank used by US forces in World War II.

HEAVY DUTY

First built to tackle foot soldiers, tanks were now designed to fight one another and their firepower and armour were increased. World War II also saw the introduction of other military vehicles, such as armoured personnel carriers.

T-34
This Russian all-purpose tank was so effective in World War II that it remained in use until 1996.

THE JEEP
Lightweight and fast, the jeep was widely used by US forces in World War II and later conflicts.

MULTI-ROLE VEHICLES

Some military vehicles are specialised for one purpose, but others can perform a variety of roles. Since World War II, old designs have been improved and new ones introduced.

SOVIET PT-76 LIGHT TANK
Introduced in the early 1950s, this tank was amphibious, enabling it to cross large rivers.

M47 PATTON
This US tank entered service in 1952 and continued in use until the late 1980s.

COLD WAR STEEL

During World War II, Soviet forces fought alongside the Allies against German troops, but not long after the war ended, a split between the Soviet Union and Western powers appeared and started to grow. This 'Cold War' drove the development of new military vehicles by both sides.

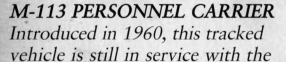

M-113 PERSONNEL CARRIER
Introduced in 1960, this tracked vehicle is still in service with the US Army today.

SOVIET T-72

TROOP MOVERS

Tanks saw significant improvements in design and other forms of vehicle began to appear. Among them were armoured troop carriers, designed to take infantry to the battle front while shielding them from fire.

FRENCH VAB APC
This vehicle is fully amphibious, propelled in water by two water jets on either side of the rear of the hull.

WATER BORNE

Another development was the appearance of military hovercraft and other amphibious vehicles. They could operate in water and on land, crossing boggy land or carrying troops from sea to shore and then across country.

1960s BELL MILITARY HOVERCRAFT

US AMPHIBIOUS ASSAULT VEHICLE

COMPLEX MACHINES

Today's military fighting machines make use of the greatest mechanical engineering technology. They are well armed and armoured, and fast, with on-board computer systems to aid targeting and navigation on the battlefield.

LEOPARD 2
This is the main battle tank of the German Army. It is also used by other countries.

FV510 WARRIOR INFANTRY SECTION VEHICLE

M'109 A6 PALADIN

The M109 was first used in the 1960s. It has been phased out by most military forces, but the US Army uses its upgraded A6 Paladin form. The M109 A6 Paladin is a highly mobile combat support weapon, which can fire shells from a distance at enemy lines. It is self-propelled, for a quick advance or retreat, and can be transported by air.

High explosive shell
— Fuse
— Explosive

Rocket-assisted shell
— Rocket motor

— Guidance equipment

XM982 Excalibur

AMMUNITION

As well as conventional, high explosive shells, the M109 A6 can fire rocket-assisted shells, which have a greater range. It also fires the XM982 Excalibur guided missile, which uses GPS targeting technology.

MAIN GUN

The 155mm howitzer has a 39-calibre M284 cannon barrel and can fire shells a distance of 30 kilometres.

Gun lock

Transmission coupling

POWER PLANT

The A6 Paladin is driven by a Detroit diesel 8V-71T engine – more powerful than that used in previous M109s.

Allison XTG-411-4 4-speed transmission

Fan

Engine guard

Detroit diesel 8V-71T

M'109 A6 PALADIN

Body length: 6.1 metres
Width: 3.1 metres
Height: 3.3 metres
Weight: 27.9 tonnes
Top speed: 61 kilometres per hour
Range without refuelling: 350 kilometres

Machine gun

Crew hatch

Reactive armour

Breech

Road wheels

THE TURRET

The large, well-armoured turret seats three crew – the gunner and two ammunition handlers. Earlier versions of the M109 needed two gunners – one to control the cannon's vertical aim and the other to control its horizontal direction. Ammunition is stored at the back of the turret.

Ammunition handler

Shell storage area

BODYWORK

The M109 is armoured with plates of rolled aluminium alloy. These are 3.2 centimetres thick.

TRACKS

The tracks are driven by the toothed front sprocket and run across seven individually sprung road wheels. The first and last of these wheels are linked to shock absorbers.

ABRAMS M1A2 MAIN BATTLE TANK

The M1 has been the world's number one tank since 1980. It is fast, mobile and quiet and is used by the US Army and the US Marines. It is named in honour of General Creighton Abrams, former Army Chief of Staff. Its quiet engine and awesome firepower have led crews to nickname it 'The Beast', 'Dracula' and 'Whispering Death'.

M1A2 ABRAMS

Body length: 7.9 metres
Width: 3.6 metres
Height to turret: 2.4 metres
Weight: 63.2 tonnes
Top speed: 67 kilometres per hour
Range without refuelling: 450 kilometres

GUN

The M256 120mm smoothbore cannon is 5.2 metres long and weighs 1.3 tonnes.

DRIVER'S STATION

The driver sits at the front and can see outside the tank by using periscopes.

Co-axial machine gun

AMMUNITION

The main gun fires a variety of ammunition, including high explosive anti-tank (HEAT) and sabot rounds. Sabot rounds do not explode but pierce the armour of enemy tanks.

Heat round

Barrel

Penetrator

Sabot round

MAIN ARMOUR

The M1A2 has 'Chobham armour', developed in the UK. It is formed from layers of steel alloy, plastics, ceramics and kevlar.

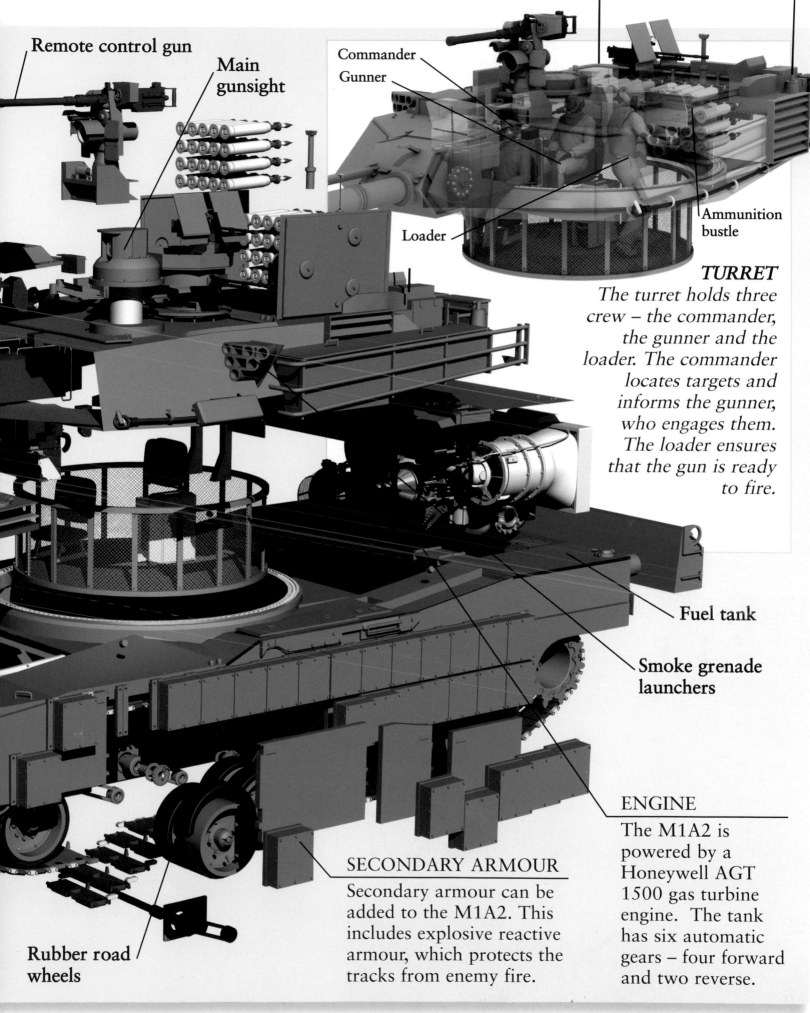

Remote control gun

Main gunsight

Commander

Gunner

Loader

Ammunition bustle

TURRET
The turret holds three crew – the commander, the gunner and the loader. The commander locates targets and informs the gunner, who engages them. The loader ensures that the gun is ready to fire.

Fuel tank

Smoke grenade launchers

Rubber road wheels

SECONDARY ARMOUR
Secondary armour can be added to the M1A2. This includes explosive reactive armour, which protects the tracks from enemy fire.

ENGINE
The M1A2 is powered by a Honeywell AGT 1500 gas turbine engine. The tank has six automatic gears – four forward and two reverse.

M270 MULTIPLE ROCKET LAUNCHER

The M270 Multiple Rocket Launcher was jointly developed by the UK, USA, Germany and France. It first went into service in 1983 and production ended in 2003, after about 1,300 units had been built. The M270 can fire up to 12 rockets in less than a minute, then move at speed to avoid returning enemy fire.

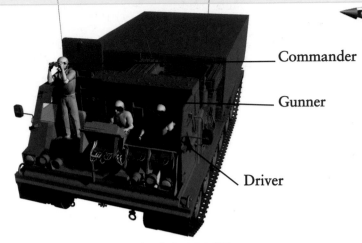

Commander

Gunner

Driver

CREW COMPARTMENT
The M270 has a crew of three, who sit up front when the rocket launcher is on the move. The crew compartment is lightly armoured to give some protection against small arms fire.

Blast shielding

ELECTRONICS
The fire control system has been upgraded since production of the M270 first began. The latest upgrades include a Global Positioning System (GPS) and local wind speed detection technology.

M270 MLRS
Body length: 6.9 metres
Width: 2.95 metres
Height: 2.6 metres
Weight (loaded): 24.8 tonnes
Top speed: 64 kilometres per hour
Range without refuelling: 480 kilometres

CHASSIS
The chassis is based on the M2 Bradley IFV (see pages 16-17). Like the M2, the M270 is as light as possible, to maximise speed.

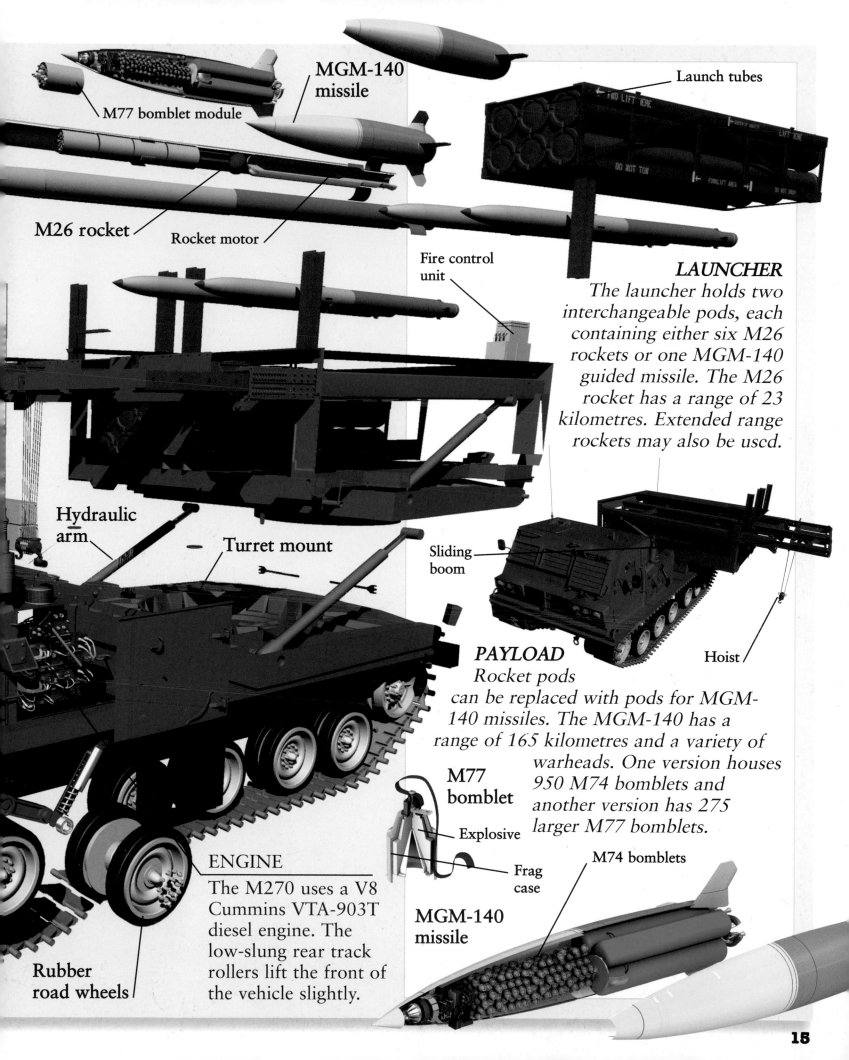

MGM-140 missile

M77 bomblet module

M26 rocket

Rocket motor

Launch tubes

Fire control unit

LAUNCHER
The launcher holds two interchangeable pods, each containing either six M26 rockets or one MGM-140 guided missile. The M26 rocket has a range of 23 kilometres. Extended range rockets may also be used.

Hydraulic arm

Turret mount

Sliding boom

Hoist

PAYLOAD
Rocket pods can be replaced with pods for MGM-140 missiles. The MGM-140 has a range of 165 kilometres and a variety of warheads. One version houses 950 M74 bomblets and another version has 275 larger M77 bomblets.

M77 bomblet

Explosive

Frag case

M74 bomblets

MGM-140 missile

ENGINE
The M270 uses a V8 Cummins VTA-903T diesel engine. The low-slung rear track rollers lift the front of the vehicle slightly.

Rubber road wheels

M2 BRADLEY IFV

The M2 Bradley IFV (Infantry Fighting Vehicle) is an armoured infantry transporter. It takes troops on to the battlefield and provides covering fire. Using its TOW (Tube-launched, Optically-tracked, Wire-guided) missile launcher, it can also destroy tanks. It was developed for the US Army to complement the Abrams M1 tank and was introduced in 1981.

Commander's viewer

TOW launcher

Main gun

ARMOUR
The M2's armour shell is aluminium, to keep it lightweight and quick. Heavier laminate and high-hardness steel armour can be added.

Bolt-on armour (lowered)

ENGINE
The M2 is powered by a V8 Cummins VTA-903T diesel engine, capable of 500 horsepower. The transmission is automatic.

Side skirts

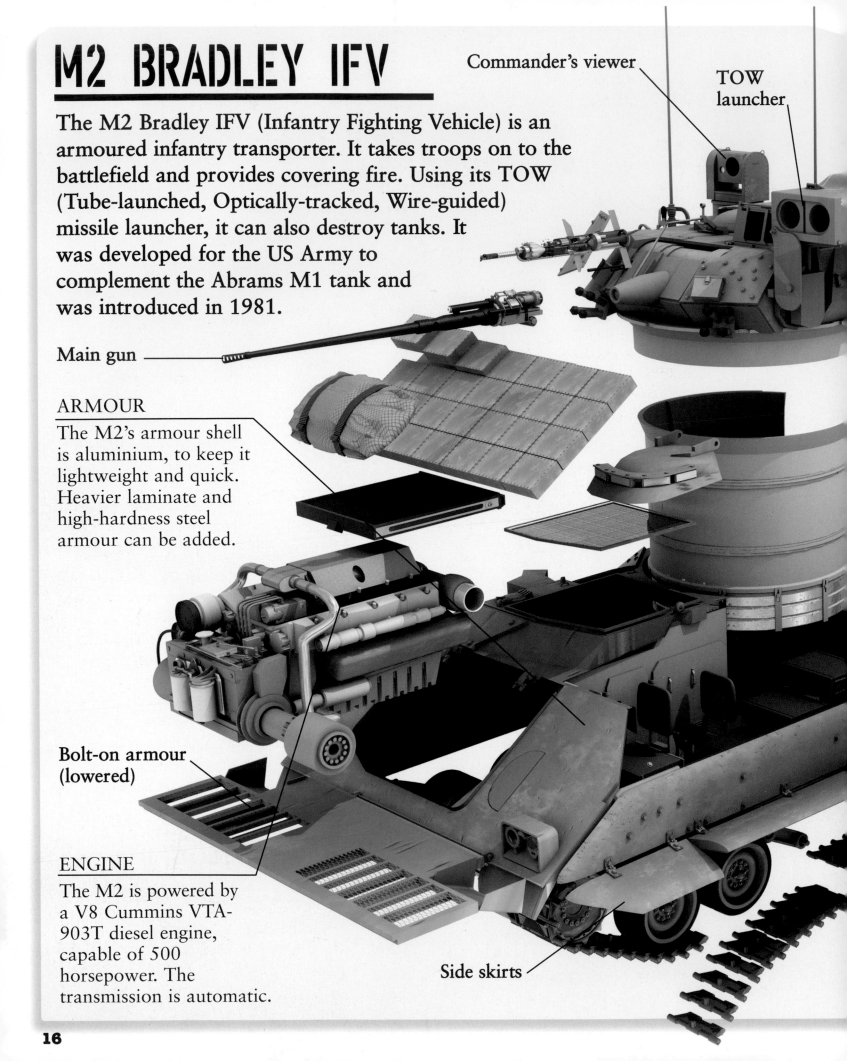

TURRET

Gunner's station

This houses the M2's commander and gunner. Hatches allow them to stand up with their upper body outside the tank, but during combat these hatches are closed. The turret is armed with a 25mm M242 chain gun and a twin tube TOW anti-tank missile launcher. The TOW launcher is used when the M2 is stationary.

M242 chain gun

Gunner

M2 BRADLEY INFANTRY FIGHTING VEHICLE

Body length: 6.7 metres
Width: 3.3 metres
Height: 3 metres
Weight: 25.5 tonnes
Top speed: 66 kilometres per hour
Range without refuelling: 483 kilometres

Warhead

TOW missile

Extendable probe

TROOP COMPARTMENT

This seats up to six fully armed soldiers. Troops enter and exit through the armoured rear door, which is hinged at the bottom.

Loading the TOW launcher

Display screen

Reactive armour

Rear door

Infantryman

WHEELS AND TRACKS

The track is driven by the front sprocket. Behind this are six dual rubber-tyre road wheels. The track itself has replaceable rubber pads for use on paved roads.

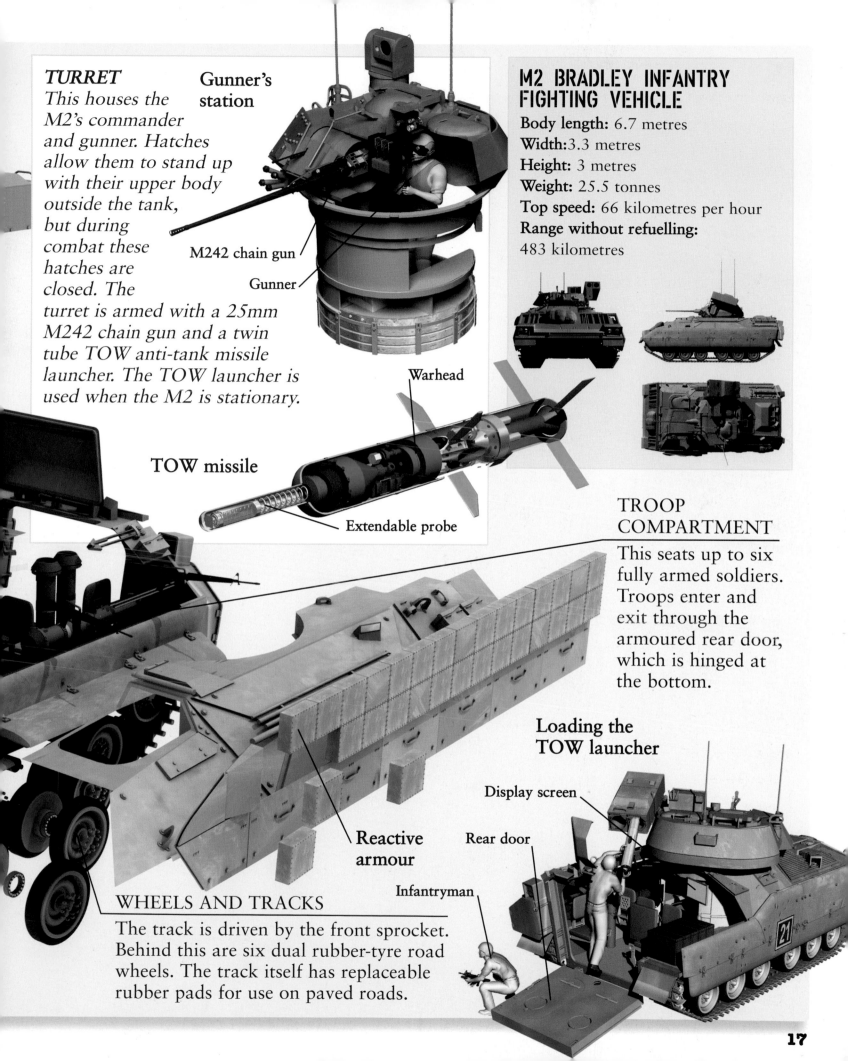

BV 206 ALL-TERRAIN CARRIER

The BV (Bandvagn) 206 is a tracked, articulated, all-terrain carrier. It was developed by the company Hägglunds for the Swedish Army and went into production in 1981. Today, the BV 206 is operated by many armed forces, including the British Army and the US Army. An armoured version is the BV 206S.

BODYWORK

The bodywork of the standard BV 206 is fire-resistant, glass-reinforced plastic. The BV 206S (shown) has additional steel armour and bulletproof glass.

DRIVER'S STATION

The driver sits in the front unit, which can also seat three passengers. The unit is insulated with PVC foam.

Engine

Wide tracks for crossing ice

ENGINE

The first BV 206 vehicles used petrol engines, but new models have Mercedes-Benz 136 hp diesels. It is mounted in the front unit and drives all four tracks.

Inline six

Turbocharger

Mercedes-Benz OM603.950 diesel engine

TRAILER

The troop-carrying trailer has space for 11 soldiers but can be adapted for carrying troops or cargo. Other variants include a mortar carrier and an anti-tank gun platform.

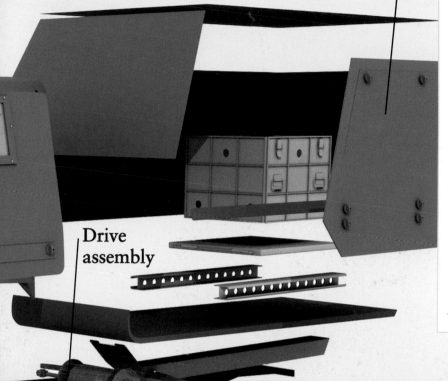

Drive assembly

ARTILLERY HUNTING RADAR

*The **ART**illery **HU**nting **R**adar system can be mounted on the trailer of the BV 206. ARTHUR uses microwaves to detect the positions and types of enemy guns. Response fire can then be rapidly co-ordinated and tracked from the trailer by the radar controllers.*

Radar

Operators' cab

ARTHUR system

Leaf-sprung track mount

WHEELS AND TRACKS

The tracks are made of moulded, reinforced rubber, unique to the BV 206, and are driven by the front-mounted sprocket, which is raised above wheel level.

LINKAGE

The linkage contains a steering unit, but is flexible, so the vehicle can easily move across rough terrain.

Powered articulated linkage

BANDVAGN 206S

Total length: 6.9 metres
Width: 1.9 metres
Height: 2.4 metres
Weight: 4.5 tonnes
Top speed: 50 kilometres per hour
Range without refuelling: 330 kilometres

HMMWV HUMVEE

The HMMWV (High-Mobility Multipurpose Wheeled Vehicle), or Humvee, is a lightweight, four-wheel drive vehicle with an automatic gearbox. It was designed for the US Army and introduced in 1985. It has been adapted to serve many functions, from field ambulance to missile launching platform.

HMMWV HUMVEE

Length: 4.6 metres
Width: 2.2 metres
Height: 1.8 metres, reducible to 1.4 metres
Weight: 2.35 tonnes
Top speed: 105 kilometres per hour
Range without refuelling: 563 kilometres

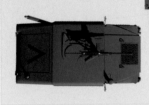

BODYWORK

The standard HMMWV bodywork is relatively lightweight, to improve its all-terrain capabilities. Additional armour is added to some models, for protection against mines and light arms.

GEP Optimizer 6500 V8

Fan

Cylinders

Gearbox

ENGINE

The HMMWV is powered by a 6.2 or 6.5 litre, fuel-injected V8 diesel engine, capable of developing up to 200 horsepower. It has an automatic gearbox with four forward and one reverse gear.

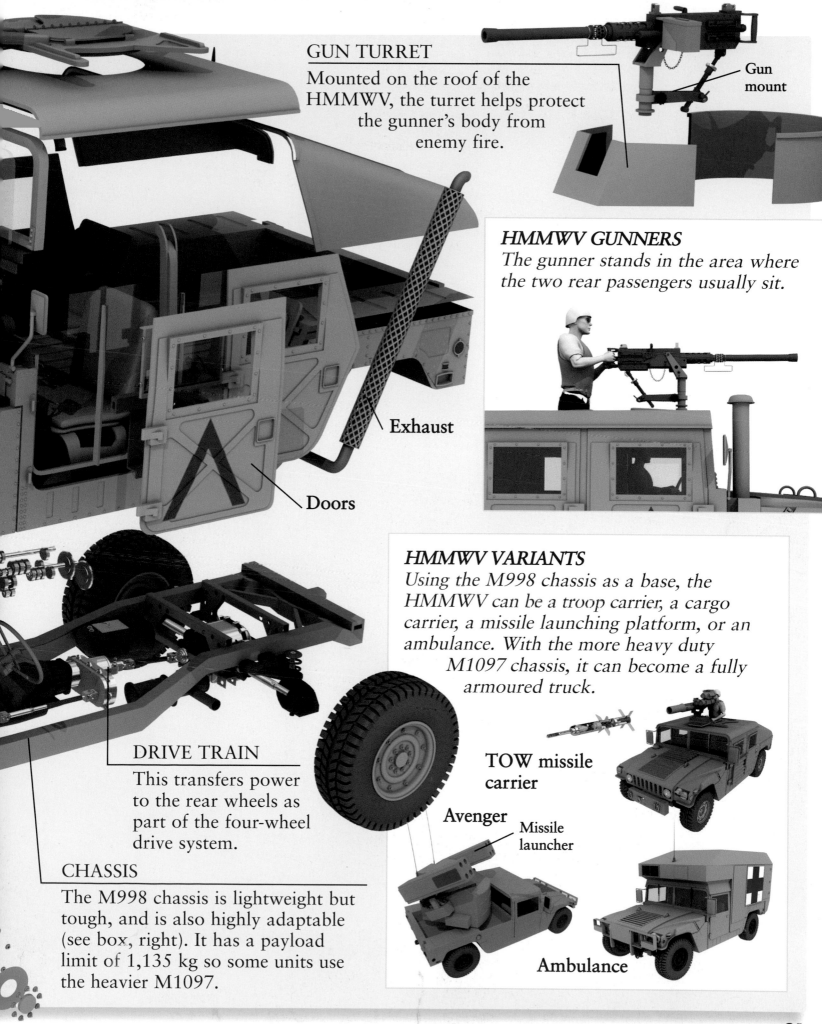

GUN TURRET

Mounted on the roof of the HMMWV, the turret helps protect the gunner's body from enemy fire.

Gun mount

Exhaust

Doors

HMMWV GUNNERS

The gunner stands in the area where the two rear passengers usually sit.

HMMWV VARIANTS

Using the M998 chassis as a base, the HMMWV can be a troop carrier, a cargo carrier, a missile launching platform, or an ambulance. With the more heavy duty M998 chassis, it can become a fully armoured truck.

TOW missile carrier

Avenger

Missile launcher

Ambulance

DRIVE TRAIN

This transfers power to the rear wheels as part of the four-wheel drive system.

CHASSIS

The M998 chassis is lightweight but tough, and is also highly adaptable (see box, right). It has a payload limit of 1,135 kg so some units use the heavier M1097.

LCAC MILITARY HOVERCRAFT

The LCAC (Landing Craft Air Cushion) military hovercraft is a high-speed vehicle used for transporting tanks, troops or equipment from the well deck of a warship to the top of a beach. First deployed in 1987, it is used by the US Navy and the Japan Maritime Self-Defence Force.

CONTROL STATION

The craftmaster and his mate sit here. The master operates the LCAC by foot pedals and a joystick control column.

Thruster

M1A2 tank

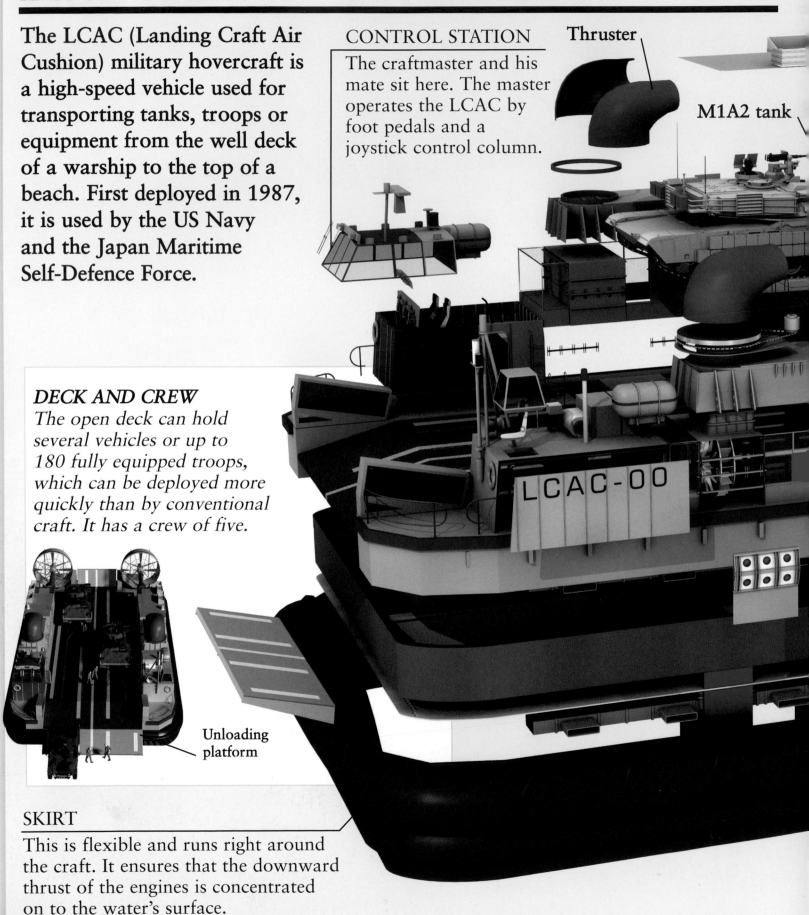

LCAC-00

DECK AND CREW

The open deck can hold several vehicles or up to 180 fully equipped troops, which can be deployed more quickly than by conventional craft. It has a crew of five.

Unloading platform

SKIRT

This is flexible and runs right around the craft. It ensures that the downward thrust of the engines is concentrated on to the water's surface.

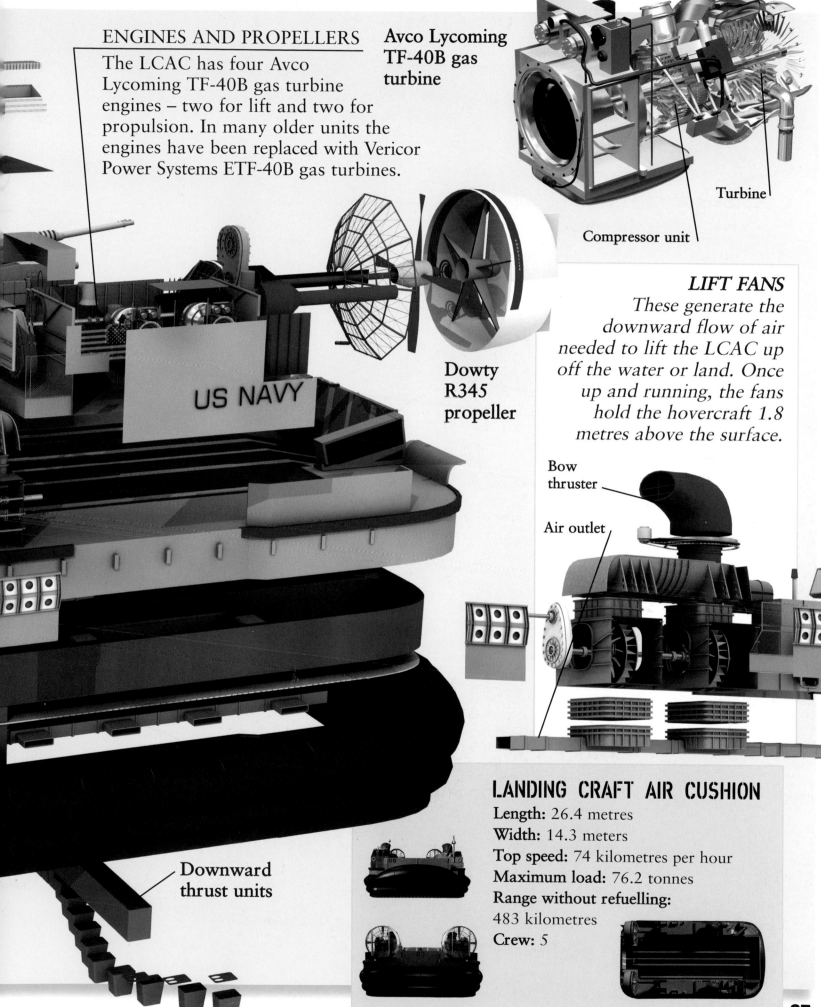

ENGINES AND PROPELLERS

The LCAC has four Avco Lycoming TF-40B gas turbine engines – two for lift and two for propulsion. In many older units the engines have been replaced with Vericor Power Systems ETF-40B gas turbines.

Avco Lycoming TF-40B gas turbine

Turbine

Compressor unit

Dowty R345 propeller

US NAVY

LIFT FANS

These generate the downward flow of air needed to lift the LCAC up off the water or land. Once up and running, the fans hold the hovercraft 1.8 metres above the surface.

Bow thruster

Air outlet

Downward thrust units

LANDING CRAFT AIR CUSHION

Length: 26.4 metres
Width: 14.3 meters
Top speed: 74 kilometres per hour
Maximum load: 76.2 tonnes
Range without refuelling: 483 kilometres
Crew: 5

M1126 STRYKER

The M1126 Stryker ICV (Infantry Carrier Vehicle) is an armoured personnel transporter. It carries soldiers into the battle zone and provides covering fire for them as they dismount and take up their positions. It was first deployed in Iraq in 2003. It is currently used exclusively by the US Army.

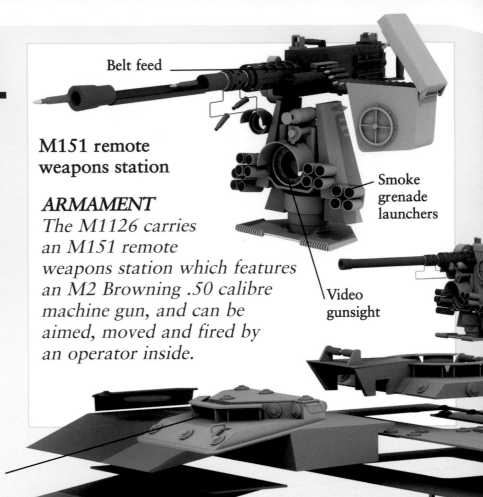

Belt feed

M151 remote weapons station

Smoke grenade launchers

Video gunsight

ARMAMENT
The M1126 carries an M151 remote weapons station which features an M2 Browning .50 calibre machine gun, and can be aimed, moved and fired by an operator inside.

Driver's hatch

ENGINE
The M1126 uses a C7 Caterpillar diesel engine. This engine is used in several other US Army vehicles, which makes running repairs easier.

Driver's station

SUSPENSION
Each of the eight wheels has independent hydropneumatic suspension. The suspension can be adjusted to lift the vehicle higher off the ground.

Drive unit

WHEELS AND TYRES
An internally controlled system alters the pressure in all eight tyres to suit terrain conditions. It can also alert the driver to a flat tyre.

ARMOUR

The armour is hard steel with lightweight ceramic layers. Inside the vehicle there is an automatic fire extinguishing system.

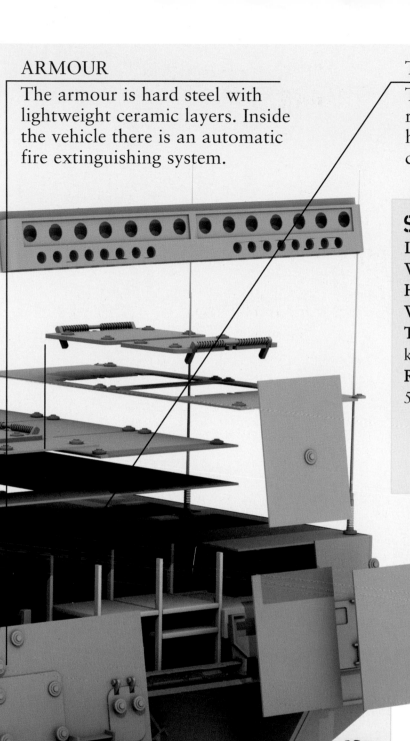

TROOP COMPARTMENT

This has space for up to nine battle ready infantry troops. The M1126 also has two crew members, the driver and commander, who stay with the vehicle.

STRYKER M1126

Length: 7 metres
Width: 2.7 metres
Height: 2.6 metres
Weight: 17.3 tonnes
Top speed: 97 kilometres per hour
Range without refuelling: 531 kilometres

M68A1 rifled cannon

M1128 MOBILE GUN SYSTEM

Unlike the M1126, which uses a M151 remote weapons station, the M1128 has a 105mm tank cannon and space for ammunition and a gun operator. The M1128 is designed to offer heavy supporting fire to infantry troops on the ground.

MRAP-COUGAR HE

The MRAP-Cougar was introduced into service in 2002. It protects its occupants from mines, small arms fire and improvised explosive devices (IEDs), such as roadside bombs. It has seen action in Iraq and Afghanistan. It is used by Canadian, British, Iraqi, Italian, Polish and US forces.

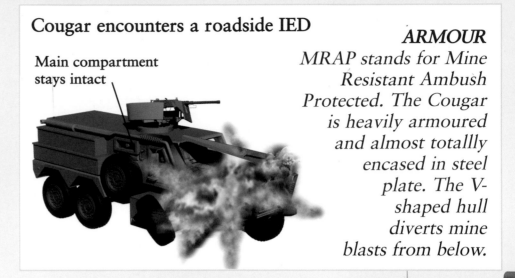

Cougar encounters a roadside IED

Main compartment stays intact

ARMOUR
MRAP stands for Mine Resistant Ambush Protected. The Cougar is heavily armoured and almost totallly encased in steel plate. The V-shaped hull diverts mine blasts from below.

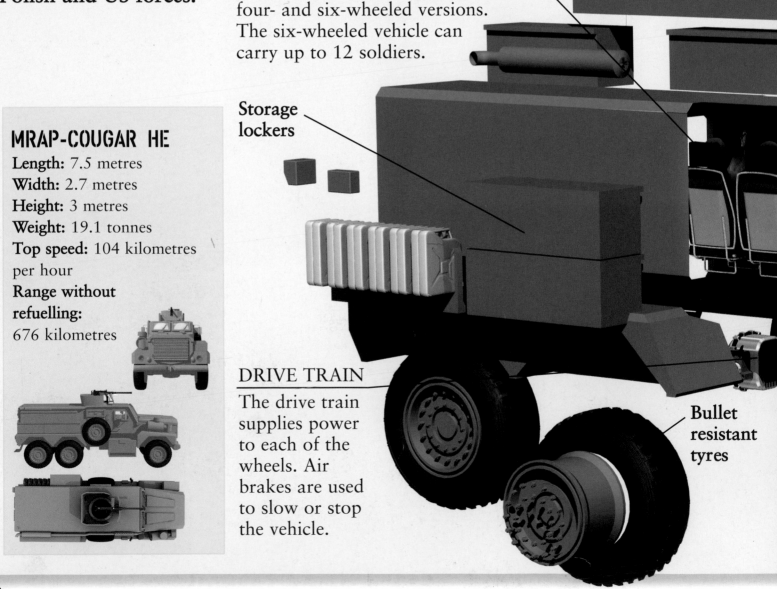

TROOP COMPARTMENT
The MRAP-Cougar comes in four- and six-wheeled versions. The six-wheeled vehicle can carry up to 12 soldiers.

Storage lockers

MRAP-COUGAR HE

Length: 7.5 metres
Width: 2.7 metres
Height: 3 metres
Weight: 19.1 tonnes
Top speed: 104 kilometres per hour
Range without refuelling: 676 kilometres

DRIVE TRAIN
The drive train supplies power to each of the wheels. Air brakes are used to slow or stop the vehicle.

Bullet resistant tyres

TROOP COMPARTMENT

This houses 17 fully equipped and combat-ready marines. Its walls are heavily armoured.

ARMOUR

The hull of the EFV is made from aluminium with mine-blast protection. The rest is covered with composite armour (consisting of layers of different material).

ENGINE

The EFV is driven by a single MT 883 Ka-523 12 cylinder diesel engine. This engine has two modes of operation – a high power mode, used for driving the vehicle at sea, and a low power mode, which is used on land. In high power mode the engine develops 2,702 horsepower.

Twin turbochargers

V12 configuration

MTU MT 883 Ka-523 turbo-diesel engine

PROPULSION SYSTEMS

At sea the EFV is propelled by waterjet propulsors, built in to either side of the hull. On land, transmission switches to the vehicle's tracks. These are covered when the EFV is in water.

GUN

The main armament of the EFV is mounted as part of the turret. It fires 200 rounds a minute and can destroy lightly armoured vehicles and aircraft, as well as enemy personnel.

Bushmaster II 30mm chain gun

Recoil spring

FUTURE MACHINES

Military technology constantly advances and vehicles are regularly replaced by new models, designed to perform most effectively in the ever-changing theatres of war.

Design programmes aim to improve both military assault and protection systems. Developing unmanned vehicles is one way of reducing the risk to fighting troops. The Armed Robotic Vehicle (ARV) is a five-tonne

UPGRADES
To save costs some machines are refitted with the latest equipment or redesigned. This BMP-1 is upgraded with a remotely operated turret.

unmanned ground vehicle with either assault or reconnaissance capabilities. Reducing energy consumption is also a priority so research is focusing on hybrid-electric technology for more efficient, powerful and versatile machines.

FUTURE COMBAT SYSTEMS
In 2010, the FCS Non-Line-Of-Sight Gun (left) will begin to replace the M109 self-propelled howitzers, currently used by the US Army.

ARMED ROBOTIC VEHICLE
Armed unmanned vehicles are becoming a reality (right). The Future Combat Systems ARV has an advanced suspension system and can venture where it is too dangerous for foot soldiers to go.

GLOSSARY

air brakes
Brakes that use compressed air to push brake pads to slow the wheels down.

amphibious
Able to operate both on land and in the water.

breech
The rear end of the barrel of a cannon or gun. In breech loading cannons, such as those used in tanks, the breech opens to allow shells to be pushed in for firing.

chassis
The rectangular steel frame that forms the skeleton of a motor vehicle. The axles and the frame that support the bodywork are attached to the chassis.

craftmaster
The captain or commanding officer of a hovercraft.

global positioning system
GPS. A system of satellites that allows people with specialised receivers to pinpoint exactly where they are on the Earth.

heavy artillery
Large calibre weapons that need a crew to operate them, firing from the ground at other surface targets.

horsepower
The amount of power transferred from a vehicle's engine to its wheels or tracks.

hydropneumatic suspension
Suspension that uses pneumatic springs filled with fluid, rather than coiled metal ones. When the pneumatic springs are compressed so is the fluid inside them.

infantry
Soldiers who fight on foot.

kevlar
A light, extremely strong synthetic fibre.

payload
The weight of people and material that a vehicle can carry.

reactive armour
Defensive armour attached to the outside of a tank or similar vehicle that reacts in some way to the impact of a shell. Explosive reactive armour contains small explosive charges that detonate when hit, helping to counteract and force away the impact of a shell.

sabot round
A bullet, shell or other round that is surrounded by a casing to increase its diameter, so it can be fired from large bore weapons. As the round leaves the barrel its casing falls away.

smoke grenade
A grenade that releases large amounts of smoke to provide cover.

sprocket
A toothed wheel.

INDEX